Glendale Library, Arts & Culture Dept.

NO LONGER PROPERTY OF
GLENDALE LIBRARY,
ARTS & CULTURE DEPT.

Habitats
Forests

Andrea Rivera

abdopublishing.com

Published by Abdo Zoom, a division of ABDO, P.O. Box 398166, Minneapolis, Minnesota 55439.

Copyright © 2018 by Abdo Consulting Group, Inc. International copyrights reserved in all countries. No part of this book may be reproduced in any form without written permission from the publisher.

Printed in the United States of America, North Mankato, Minnesota.
092017
012018

THIS BOOK CONTAINS RECYCLED MATERIALS

Photo Credits: iStock, Shutterstock

Production Contributors: Kenny Abdo, Jennie Forsberg, Grace Hansen, John Hansen

Design Contributors: Dorothy Toth, Neil Klinepier

Publisher's Cataloging-in-Publication Data

Names: Rivera, Andrea, author.

Title: Forests / by Andrea Rivera.

Description: Minneapolis, Minnesota: Abdo Zoom, 2018. | Series: Habitats | Includes online resource and index.

Identifiers: LCCN 2017939235 | ISBN 9781532120657 (lib.bdg.) | ISBN 9781532121777 (ebook) | ISBN 9781532122330 (Read-to-Me ebook)

Subjects: LCSH: Forests--Juvenile literature. | Biomes--Juvenile literature. | Habitats--Juvenile literature.

Classification: DDC 577.3--dc23

LC record available at https://lccn.loc.gov/2017939235

Table of Contents

Science.................................4

Technology 10

Engineering 14

Art...................................... 16

Math 18

Key Stats 20

Glossary.............................. 22

Online Resources.................. 23

Index 24

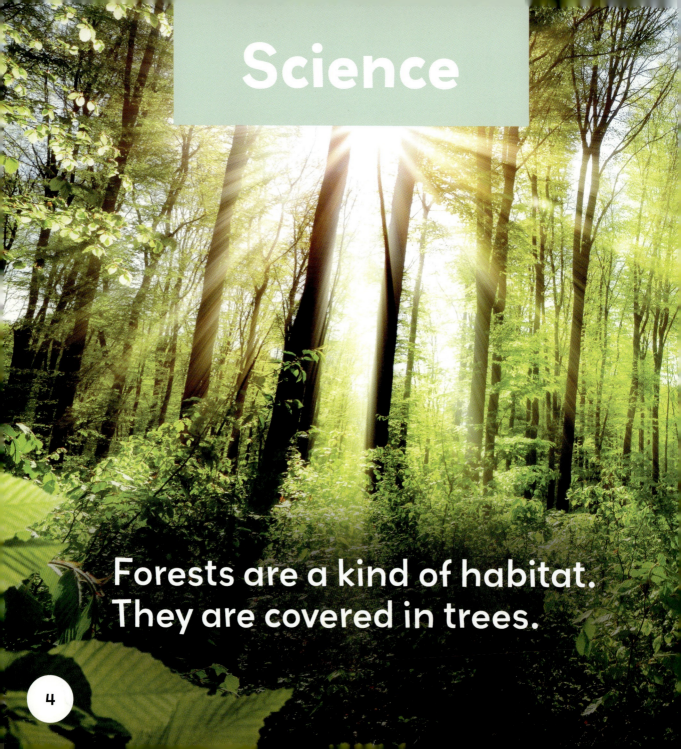

Science

Forests are a kind of habitat. They are covered in trees.

Many other plants grow in forests too.

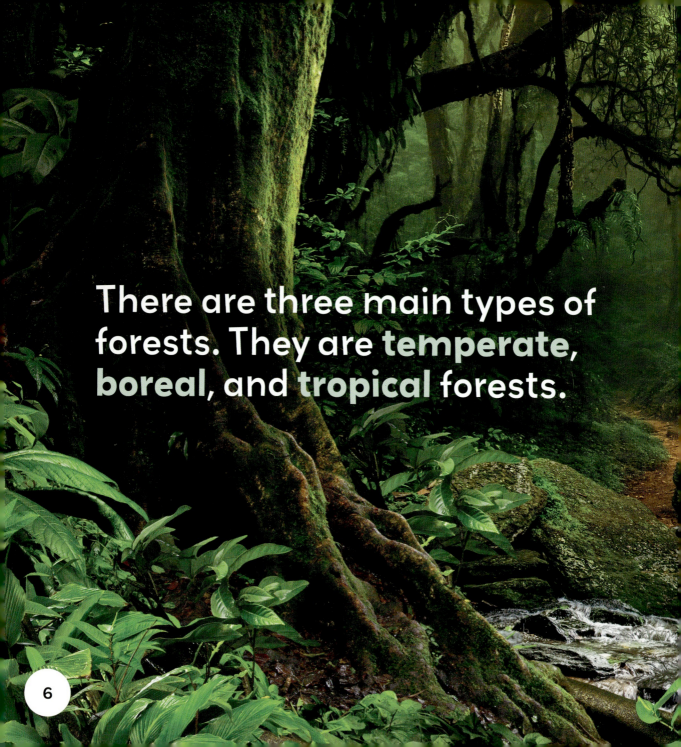

There are three main types of forests. They are **temperate, boreal,** and **tropical** forests.

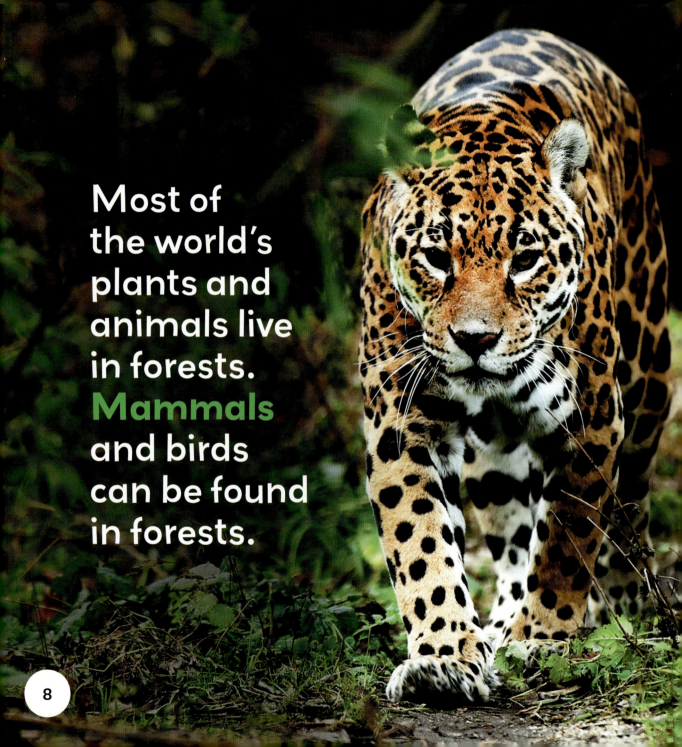

Most of the world's plants and animals live in forests. **Mammals** and birds can be found in forests.

Many reptiles, amphibians, and insects live in forests too!

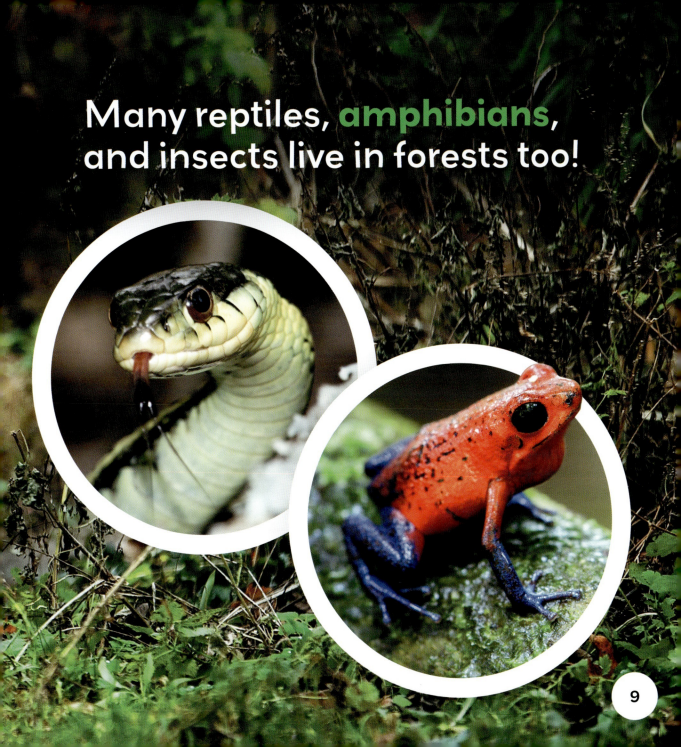

Technology

Trees from forests can be turned into paper.

First the trees are chopped down. The trees are cut into small wood chips.

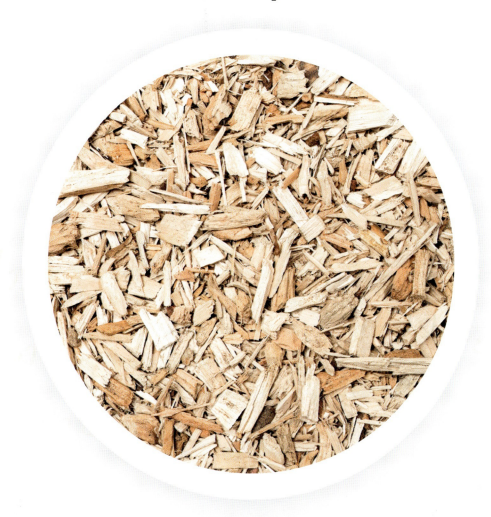

The wood chips are broken down into a pulp.

The pulp goes into a machine. Rollers press it and dry it. Paper comes out!

Engineering

Forest **engineers** work to keep these habitats healthy.

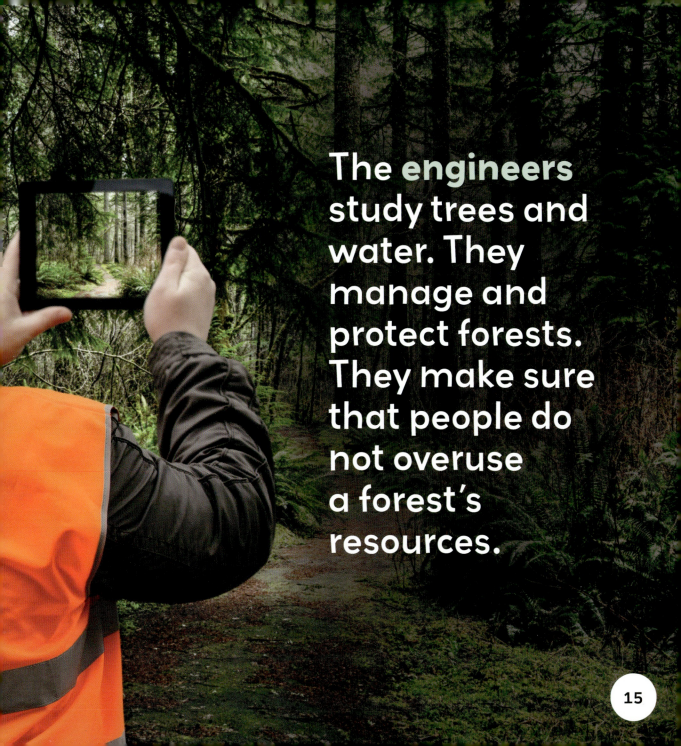

The **engineers** study trees and water. They manage and protect forests. They make sure that people do not overuse a forest's resources.

Art

Totem poles are traditional Native American monuments. A tree is chosen from a forest. Designs are carved into the tree. Then it is painted.

Math

You can tell a tree's age from the stump's rings. Each ring is equal to one year. The largest tree in the world is in California. It is more than 2,000 years old!

- Forests cover about one-third of the land on Earth.

- **Boreal** forests grow in the north. **Temperate** forests grow in places with mild temperatures. **Tropical** forests grow in hot, rainy areas.

- Rain forests are important. They can be temperate or tropical.

- Tropical rain forests have more than half of the species on Earth.

Glossary

amphibian – a small animal that hatches in the water and has gills, but later grows lungs to breathe air.

boreal – northern forests consisting mostly of pine and spruce trees.

engineer – one who is trained to use or design certain technologies.

mammal – a warm-blooded animal with fur or hair on its skin and a skeleton inside its body.

temperate – a forest that experiences four seasons.

tropical – a hot, moist forest located near the equator.

Online Resources

For more information on forests, please visit **abdobooklinks.com**

Learn even more with the Abdo Zoom STEAM database. Visit **abdozoom.com** today!

Index

animals 8, 9

boreal 6

California 19

engineer 14, 15

insects 9

Native American 16

paper 10, 11, 13

plants 5, 8

temperate 6

totem pole 16

tree 4, 10, 11, 15, 16, 19

tropical 6

water 15